A portrait of a dancer and a ballet in the making

NUREYEV IN PARIS

NUREYEV
IN
PARIS

LE JEUNE HOMME ET LA MORT

PHOTOGRAPHED BY JURGEN VOLLMER

A portrait of a dancer, Rudolf Nureyev, and of a ballet, *Le Jeune Homme et la Mort*. Choreographed by Roland Petit, with a scenario by Jean Cocteau and setting by George Wakhevitch. Danced by Rudolf Nureyev and Zizi Jeanmaire.

TEXT BY JOHN DEVERE
DESIGNED BY JURGEN VOLLMER AND JOHN DEVERE

a modernismo book

THE CONCEPT

Artistic freedom as a dancer was Rudolf Nureyev's goal, and he left the Kirov Ballet and Russia in order to achieve it. During his years in the West, he has enthusiastically added modern dance roles to his extensive classical repertory, roles conceived by Jose Limon, Paul Taylor, George Balanchine, Maurice Bejart. When French choreographer Roland Petit invited Nureyev to Paris to dance *Le Jeune Homme et la Mort*, it provided Nureyev an opportunity to dance in a ballet that was itself a hybrid crossing of classical ballet idiom and modern dance vocabulary. Petit's *Le Jeune Homme et la Mort*, its scenario originally conceived by Jean Cocteau in 1946 and choreographed to a Bach Passacaglia, was filmed for French television, starring Nureyev and Zizi Jeanmaire.

IN PREPARATION

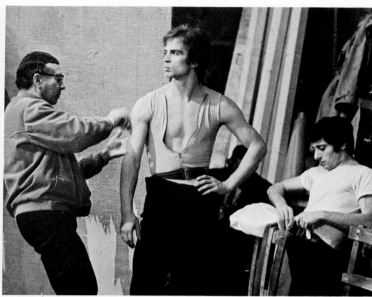

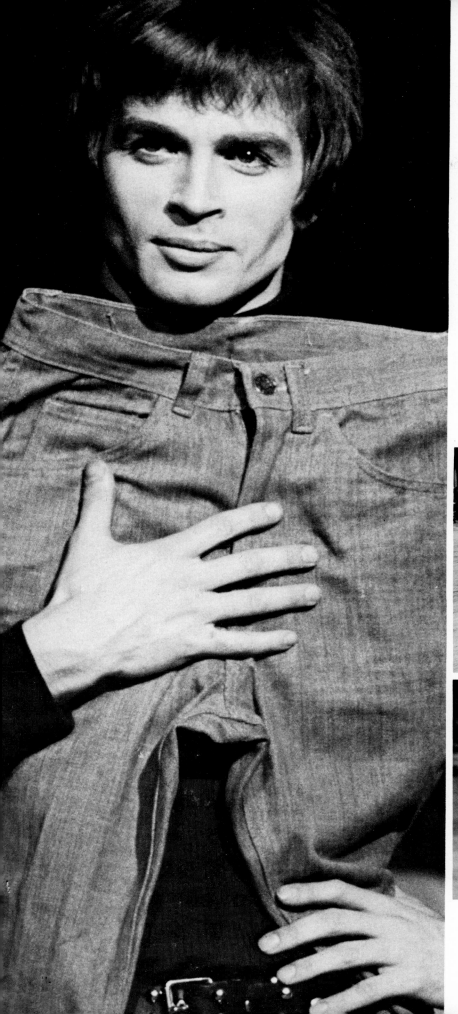

From initial discussions through rehearsals to finished performance, photographer Jurgen Vollmer lensed this ballet in the making. In the process, he captured a unique portrait of Nureyev at work, the man behind the myth. His photo chronicle is in fact a documentary, behind-the-scenes study of creative collaboration, of artistic discipline, of dance intensity. From make-up, costume and lighting tests, on these pages, to the finished ballet, Vollmer photographed the bits and pieces of an entire artistic mosaic. His photographs form therefore an ensemble, not a mere collection: a portrait of a dancer and a ballet.

THE EXERCISES

At the barre, warming up, Nureyev demostrates the classical technique at the core of his Russian training: exhaustive daily discipline, the behind-the-scenes effort that results in seeming effortlessness on stage.

THE EXERCISES

Nureyev has always seemed to incarnate Nietzsche's conception of art as a precarious balance between Dionysian intensity and the restrained, ordered mask of Apollo. If classical dance is ideally Apollonian, Nureyev's personal undercurrents of Dionysian vitality add an extra intensity to everything he undertakes. That intensity is particularly appropriate to *Le Jeune Homme et la Mort*

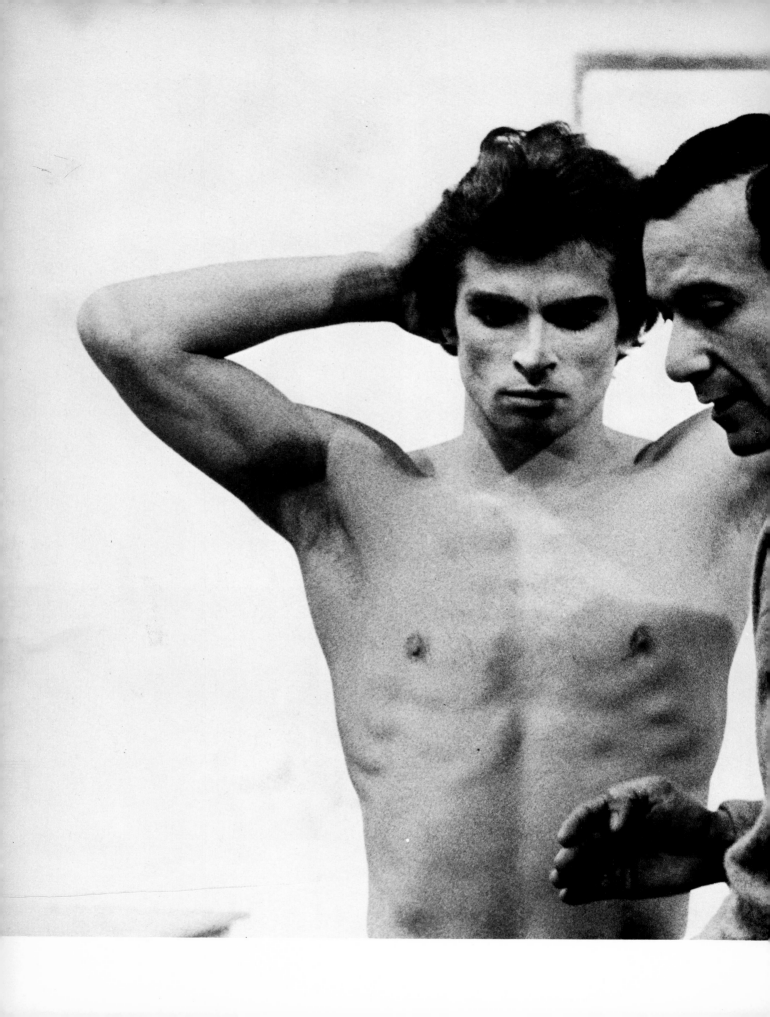

COLLABORATION

Every ballet role is, of course, subtly modified by the individual nuances different dancers bring to it. *Le Jeune Homme et la Mort*, originally conceived by Petit for Jean Babillee in 1946, was rechoreographed for Nureyev. His personal dynamism added new dimensions to the character of "le jeune homme," tortured by erotic frustrations and dark psychological demons, a role requiring as much acting ability as dance virtuosity. In initial sessions, choreographer Roland Petit and dancer Zizi Jeanmaire explored every nuance of the ballet with Nureyev.

IN REHEARSAL

In the mirror, his image mimicks him. Nureyev, rehearsing with piano, finds the ballet's pace, its pulse.

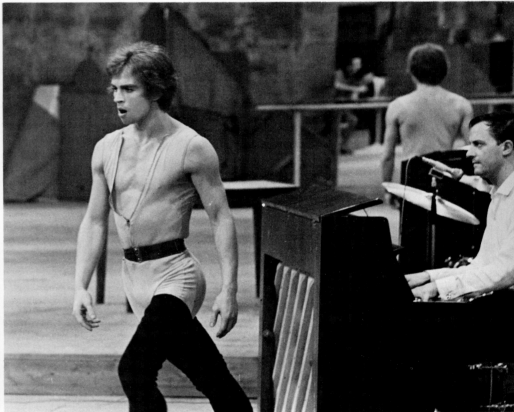

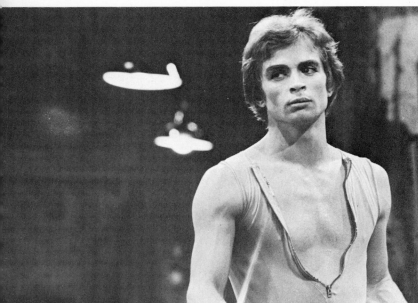

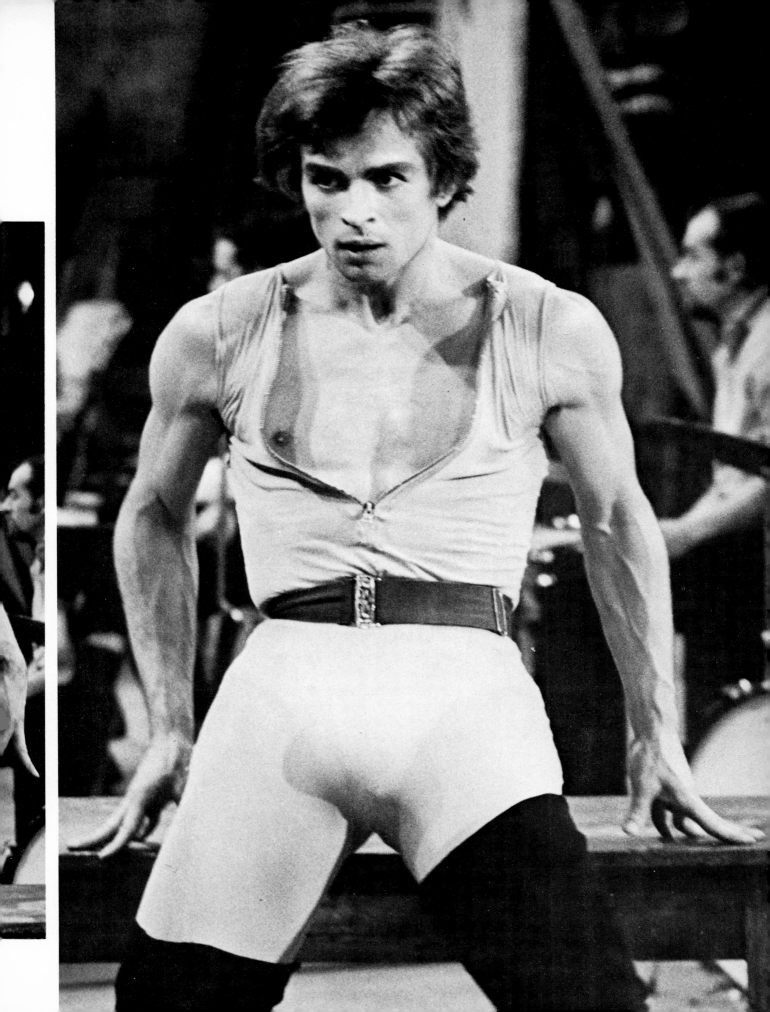

CONCENTRATION

Moods change kaleidoscopically, as Nureyev and Jeanmaire collaborate. Hours of fierce concentration, of self-conscious stage awareness, alternate with moments of abstraction and self-absorption. Conceptualizing plays as vital a part in dance realization as does the more visceral immediacy of actual physical accomplishment; Nureyev is as intellectual in his approach to dance as he is instinctive. His extraordinary ability to make the carefully rehearsed seem entirely spontaneous accounts for the electricity he generates.

COMIC RELIEF

Rehearsal and performance pressures yield to comic relief, as Nureyev, Jeanmaire and Petit break their concentration on *Le Jeune Homme et la Mort* for lively camaraderie.

IN PERFORMANCE

As originally conceived by Jean Cocteau, *Le Jeune Homme et la Mort* reflects two distinctly discernable, yet radically different, influences: Romanticism and existentialism. The neo-Romantic tradition links, inextricably, love and death. This nineteenth century fascination with *eros* and *thanatos*, the life impulse and the death wish, culminated with the "Liebestod" in Wagner's *Tristan und Isolde*, literally a "lovedeath." The theme carried over into the twentieth century with Thomas Mann's *Death in Venice*. If the ballet's roots are in Romanticism, a more immediate influence, both philosophical and esthetic, is the

existentialist atmosphere of post-World War II Paris, with its emphasis on subjective despair, disillusionment and desperation. *Le Jeune Homme et la Mort* is thus firmly rooted in French literary traditions.

SOLITUDE

In his garret room, a young man, alone and lonely, restlessly awaits his lover. When she does not appear, his poetic melancholy metamorphoses into frenzied erotic frustration.

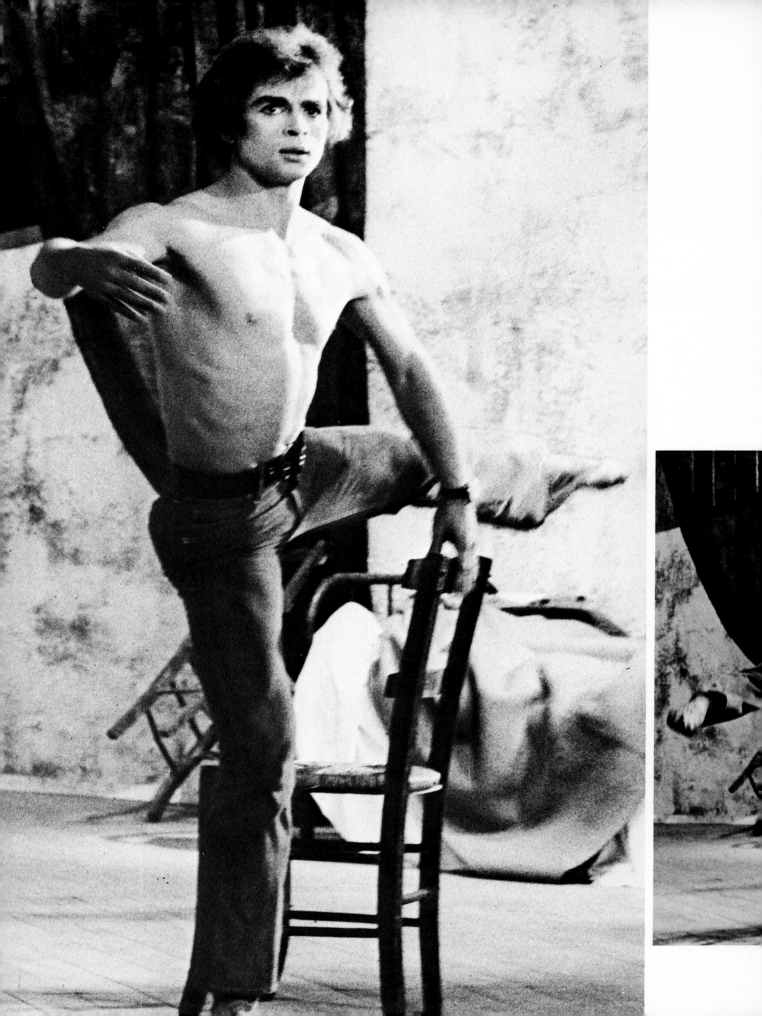

FRUSTRATION

Anguished, the young man externalizes his solitude in a dance soliloquy of increasing despair and desolation, its muscular frenzy mirroring his psychological turbulence.

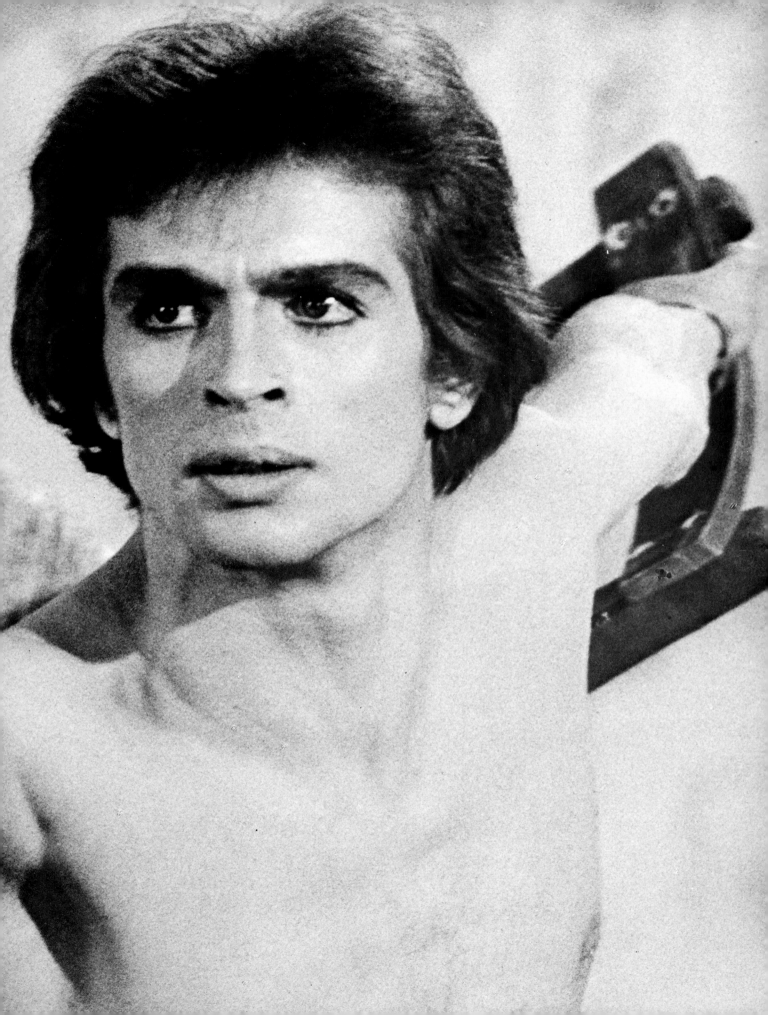

FEMME FATALE

The lover arrives.

She is starkly glacial, a dark malevolence, literally a *femme fatale*. As *la belle dame sans merci*, she too has provocative antecedents — Mallarme's Herodiade, Flaubert's Salammbo, Wilde's and Strauss' Salome, Puccini's Turandot, and Tschiakovsky's black swan Odile — those ice princesses who beguile, leading or misleading their lovers in a destiny toward darkness. They seduce in order to betray. They promise *eros*; they deliver *thanatos*.

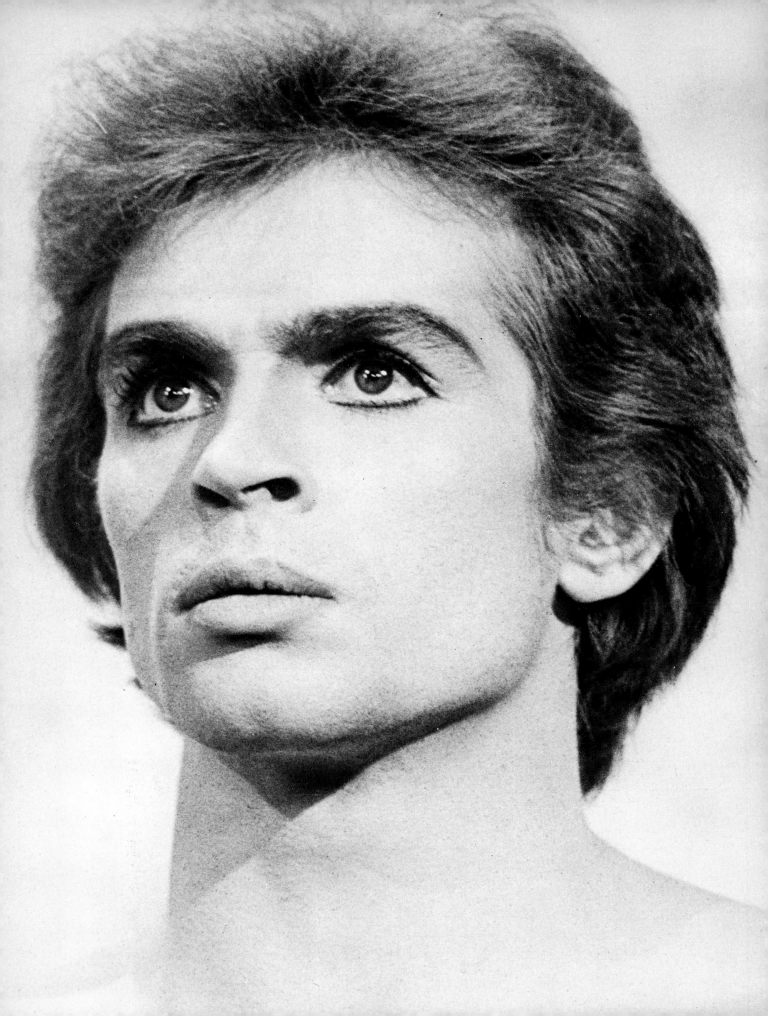

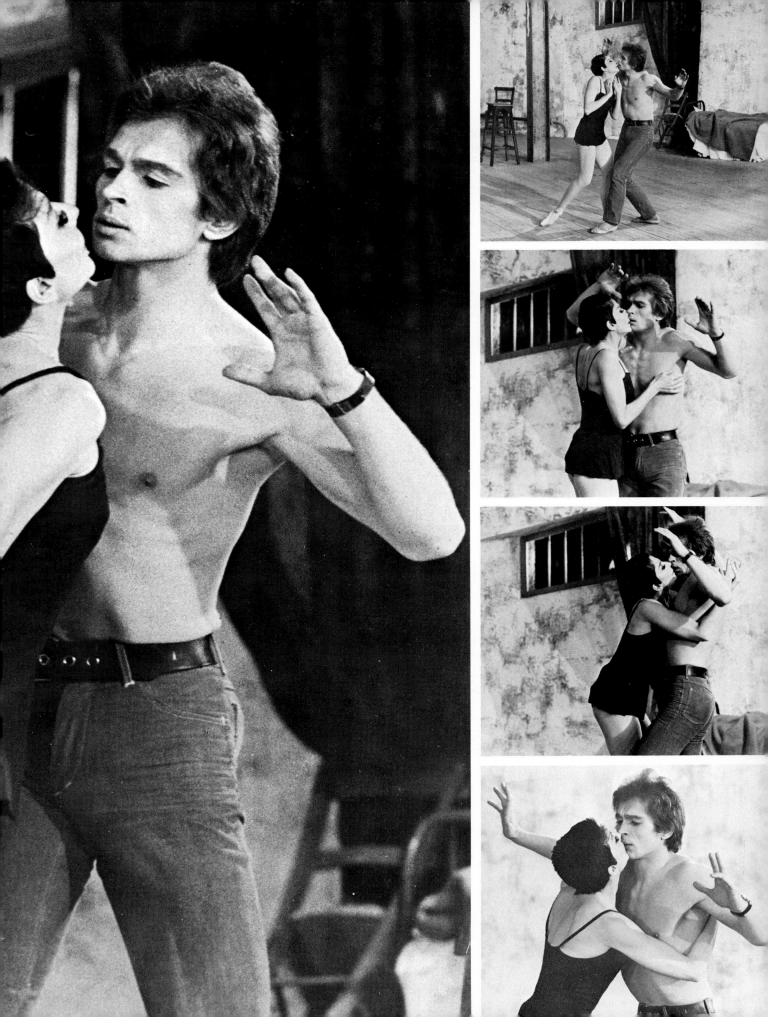

Tantalizingly seductive yet unattainable, touching yet untouchable, the lover plays a fierce and deadly sensual game. The young man's anguish is in fact the "Romantic agony," that tragic realization of the discrepancy between desire and actuality,

SEDUCTION AND BETRAYAL

between subjective dream and objective possibility.

The lover's taunting escalates, culminates in hostility, in antagonism, in violence. And if her tenderness recommences, it is only in order to effect the ultimate betrayal.

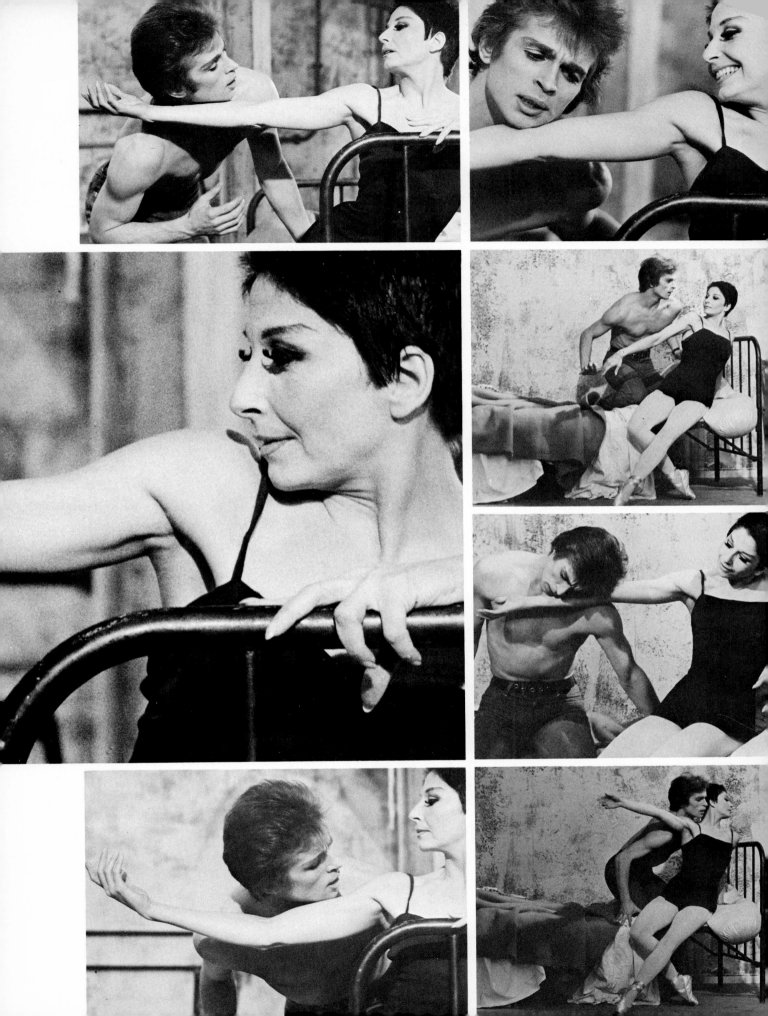

VIOLENCE

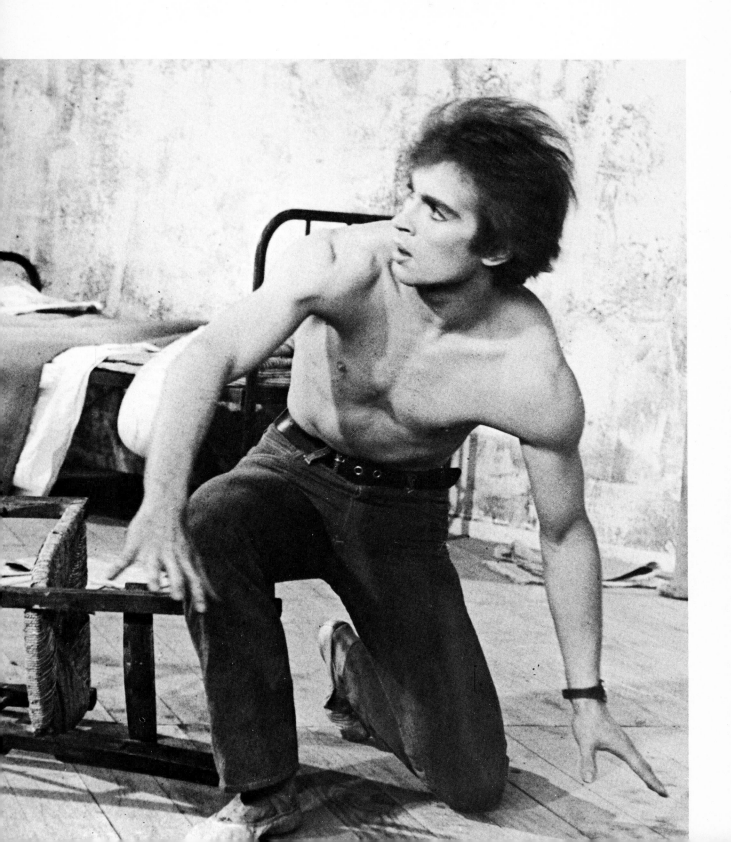

EROS AND THANATOS

The fatal collision of archetypes
— the collision of this questing,
poetic youth, this melancholy
Werther, with the all-consuming,
intransigent female principle —
links, in the French tradition,
l'amour and *la mort*. The demon
lover prepares the noose,
suspending it from an exposed
beam in the young man's garret.
This *femme fatale* is Death itself.
As she points toward the ultimate

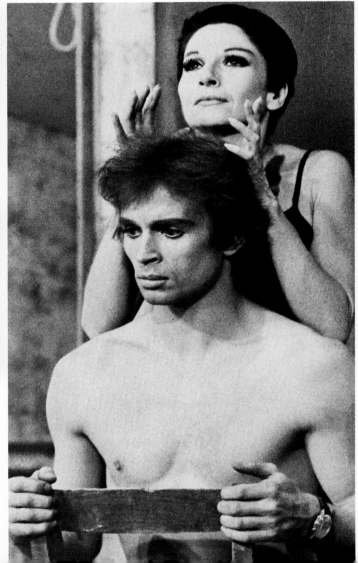

outlet for his despair, *Le Jeune Homme et la Mort* takes its place in the poetically self-destructive traditions of both Romanticism and existentialism. The lover's final embrace is not the embrace of eros, *l'amour*, but of thanatos, *la mort.*

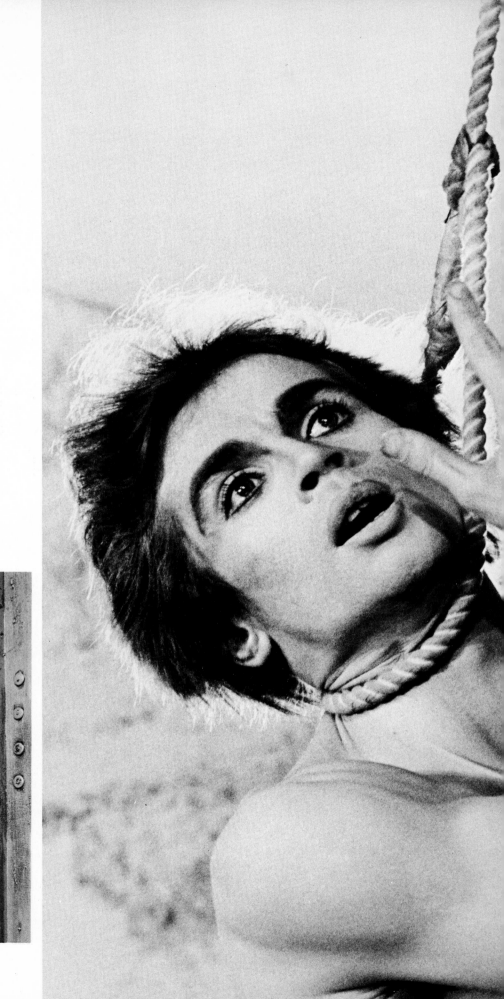